# MATT RAWLE

Author of *The Redemption of Scrooge*

# THE GRACE OF
*Les Misérables*

## LEADER GUIDE

by Ben Simpson

Abingdon Press/Nashville

### The Grace of *Les Misérables*
### Leader Guide

*Copyright © 2019 Abingdon Press*
*All rights reserved.*

ISBN 978-1-5018-8712-3

19 20 21 22 23 24 25 26 27 28 — 10 9 8 7 6 5 4 3 2 1
MANUFACTURED IN THE UNITED STATES OF AMERICA

# CONTENTS

# A NOTE TO GROUP LEADERS

Victor Hugo's *Les Misérables* is a classic, best-selling book that has entered our collective imagination not only in the form of the novel, but also as a play, a major motion picture, and a musical. Published in 1862, the book was and is celebrated as one of the greatest novels of the nineteenth century. It continues to sell. Its popularity has endured. The 2012 film adaptation that was nominated for several Academy Awards stars Hugh Jackman, Russell Crowe, and Anne Hathaway. There have been anime and manga adaptations, and a television miniseries based on the story appeared as recently as 2019.

Why has this story persisted? *Les Misérables* is immense in scope, exploring themes of law and grace, the history of France, and the charm of Paris. But there is more: The characters in *Les Misérables* each represent a different idea, such as grace, justice, poverty, and love. The real gift of Hugo's story is to see how these ideas interact. For example, what does it look like when grace and justice collide? Is revolution the best answer to solving the human invention of poverty? Does love really win in the end? One could spend a lifetime discussing the themes in *Les Mis*.

In *The Grace of Les Misérables*, Matt Rawle invites us to examine these themes through the lens of Christian faith. He does so via the characters, settings, and major plot elements of Victor Hugo's *Les Misérables* novel. Matt invites us to see beyond a familiar story in order to discover God's graceful narrative that sometimes hides just beneath the surface.

As a group leader, your role is to facilitate weekly sessions using

- the Bible,
- Matt Rawle's *The Grace of Les Misérables* (page references throughout this Leader Guide are to Matt's book),
- this Leader Guide, and
- the accompanying DVD or streaming video.

This Leader Guide includes instructions on how to structure a sixty-minute session. Each session opens with a lesson aim, a few themes to develop, a primary selection from the Bible, and a quotation from the author that identifies a major theological idea.

There are three major movements for each session in the study:

- Gather;
- Grow in Grace: Video, Book, and Scripture; and
- Go: Equipped to Serve the World.

The first and last sections should take about ten minutes each, while the second section should receive the majority of your focus as you discuss the video, book, and a passage from Scripture.

Make sure to read through each session prior to gathering. Consider your words carefully, and if you know the participants, prayerfully consider what points of discussion will be most helpful for them. The goal is to help each person take a next step in their faith life. This Leader Guide contains plenty of choices for your session, so you will need to be selective if you wish to go deep on one or two discussion questions or if you think it would be best to spend an extended period of time engaged with the Scripture. Come to each session prayerfully prepared.

Last, by leading this study you are being faithful to Jesus' command to teach and disciple others. You are demonstrating grace to other participants—hopefully because you have begun to realize how gracious Jesus has been to you. Lives can be changed in this study. Pay attention as God works. Put what you learn into action. Respond to God's grace with faith, and in faith, take action. Live according to the measure of grace given you. In Jesus, that's more than you can imagine.

## Session 1

# GRACE WELL RECEIVED: THE STORY OF JEAN VALJEAN

## SESSION OVERVIEW

### Introduction

The story of Jean Valjean is powerful because it demonstrates how grace can be well received. Valjean was a hardened criminal. But an act of grace changed him, which began a journey of transformation throughout the rest of his life.

Like Jean Valjean, we are recipients of grace. Jesus has graciously loved us, graciously redeemed us, and graciously seeks to sanctify us. How do we respond? Do we receive God's grace well?

### Lesson Aim

*To define grace as God's free, loving action toward us,
exhibited most fully in Jesus Christ,
and to choose to live in response to God's grace*

7

## Session Themes

- To examine Jean Valjean's story and what it teaches us about grace;
- To reflect on moments of grace in our own lives;
- To accept God's grace given to us in Jesus and to worship as a response to God's love;
- To commit to acts of grace, love, and kindness toward those around us: friends, family, coworkers, strangers, and enemies.

## Chapter Focus: Jean Valjean

In each chapter, Matt Rawle explores characters, settings, and themes from *Les Misérables* to illustrate important biblical and theological truths. In this session, focus your group on the example of Jean Valjean, whose life was transformed by grace.

Jean Valjean experiences transformation following an encounter with a priest named Bishop Myriel. Myriel welcomed Valjean, who had been released from jail, and offered him a place to rest. At night, while the household was sleeping, Valjean stole the bishop's silverware and fled. He was caught. Rather than press charges, the bishop covered for him and offered him his silver candlesticks, telling the authorities he had offered them, along with the silverware, to Valjean in order to get him back on his feet. Valjean did not understand the bishop's actions, but neither could he shake their consequences. Valjean had been given a gift. How would he respond?

## Key Scripture

> *By grace you have been saved through faith, and this is not your own doing; it is the gift of God—not the result of works, so that no one may boast. For we are what he has made us, created in Christ Jesus for good works, which God prepared beforehand to be our way of life.*
>
> *(Ephesians 2:8-10)*

## Theological Focus

The popular musical based on Hugo's story suggests that Valjean's conversion from criminal to saint happens in the blink of an eye, and his commitment to following a holy path becomes an almost instinctual action. The original story, however, suggests that choosing the good is a daily and often difficult choice. Much like a recovering addict, Valjean struggles with dampening his personal demons for the sake of making holy choices. If we are honest, our story is similar. Always choosing the good would be easy if the good were obvious. Jean Valjean's journey helps us recognize how difficult accepting grace can be, and how sharing grace can sometimes be even more difficult.

*(Rawle, p. 18)*

# GATHER (10 MINUTES)

Welcome the group to the study. Introduce yourself and learn the names of all group participants if you do not know everyone. Allow time for group members to become acquainted.

Start by asking the group:

- How familiar are you with *Les Misérables*?
- If you are familiar with *Les Misérables*, when did you first encounter it?
- Why, do you think, did Matt Rawle choose *Les Misérables* as the subject of a Bible study? What does this story have to teach Christians?

In the first session, share the overview of the plot, characters, and timeline of *Les Misérables*. Share with the group that each session will include discussion, prayer, a video where you will hear from Matt Rawle, a close look at the book, and an examination of Scripture in light of the theme. Tell the group that *together* you will look for ways to apply what you have learned and challenge one another to live in light of the good news revealed in Jesus.

## Opening Prayer

*Gracious God, you have demonstrated great love for us in Jesus. Help us today to learn how better to respond to your grace, discerning right from wrong. Then, may we boldly take action in light of the good gifts we have received from you. Amen.*

## Conversation Starter

**Say:**

The first chapter in our book explores the theme of grace through an examination of the character of Jean Valjean. Grace is one of the major themes of the Bible and an important aspect of Christian theology and practice. What, then, is grace? As Matt Rawle writes, "Grace is offered even before we are aware we are in need, it justifies us so that we can stop justifying ourselves, and it is the power of God to transform who we are. Sometimes this gift takes a lifetime to recognize" (p. 39). How has God shown grace to you? to us? to the world? How does God call us to live in light of the grace we have received through Jesus? Choosing to consistently act in light of the grace we have received can be very difficult. Today we will discuss how following Jesus deepens our understanding of grace and transforms us into gracious people.

**Ask and discuss:**

- Can you think of a contemporary story in which someone was in need of grace? What happened? How was this person changed by grace? Was grace even offered? What was the result?
- What is grace? How does God demonstrate and extend grace to us? What difference does God's grace make in daily Christian living?

# GROW IN GRACE: VIDEO, BOOK, AND SCRIPTURE (40 MINUTES)

*This section allows approximately thirty minutes for discussion of the book and Scripture after the video portion concludes. You will not have time to address every discussion question. Select questions in advance you believe will be most helpful for your group and address those questions first. It may help to put a checkmark by the questions you want to cover. If time allows, incorporate additional questions.*

## Watching the Video

**Say:**

> We will continue our time together with a video featuring Matt Rawle. Matt will talk about the primary theme of this first chapter: grace and Jean Valjean. Notice how he explains this theme. Make connections to what we have read together in his book. Then, we will discuss both the video and our book together.

**Play the video:** Session I on Valjean (approximately 10 minutes)

**Say:**

> Let's keep what Matt has said in mind as we take a look at the book and examine these themes in light of our calling to live as disciples of Jesus.

## The Book

Chapter 1 explores the theme of grace as seen in the life of Jean Valjean. Rawle invites us to reflect on how God has been gracious to us and how we should respond.

**Choose from the questions below for your discussion:**

- Matt Rawle writes, "*Les Misérables* is a story that wrestles with the intersection between offering grace and maintaining justice" (p. 19). What is the connection between grace and justice for a follower of Christ? How does the grace of God lead us to work for justice?
- Rawle asks, "Have you ever been in a situation where there is tension between the means and the end, or doing something that might stretch the rules to the point of breaking, but goodness was the end result?" (p. 20). Rawle cites Monseigneur Myriel, a priest, as an example of someone who did so, and Rawle also shows where Jesus challenged convention and asked his opponents to rethink the story of God. Have you ever faced a situation where you challenged convention because of a "good" you were seeking to achieve?
- Rawle explains how Jean Valjean became a criminal. His family fell into poverty and was starving, he stole bread to meet their needs, and he was caught. Marked afterward as a thief, he was ostracized, hardening his heart further, pushing him to again break the law. What questions does Valjean's experience raise about the nature of justice? about compassion? about the shape of a healthy society?
- Valjean encounters Monseigneur Myriel, or M. Bienvenu. Myriel offers Valjean hospitality. Rawle connects this encounter with Jesus' parable of the prodigal son, found in Luke 15:11-32. How is Myriel like the father in that parable? How is Valjean like the younger son?
- Valjean responds to Myriel's hospitality by stealing his silver and attempting to escape in the middle of the night. Valjean does not receive grace with gratitude, but with greediness. Rawle reminds us that grace is not always reciprocated and that Jesus told us not to expect a return for the good we do, but instead to bless others freely. Why is this difficult for us to understand and apply? How does grace reshape our expectations for others?

- Rawle writes, "The local police apprehend Valjean for stealing the priest's silver in the middle of the night, and when M. Bienvenu is invited to identify Valjean as the thief, the priest surprises everyone. He offers Valjean additional silver, claiming that what Valjean had taken was a gift. After Valjean is released, M. Bienvenu tells Valjean that he must use this silver to become an honest man. This act of kindness is almost too much for Valjean to bear" (pp. 23–24). Why was this act of grace so unsettling for Valjean? How does this instance in the *Les Mis* story connect to the Christian story? How does grace unsettle us and reform us?
- Rawle writes, "Following Christ is more than avoiding sin or evading things that distract us from loving God and loving our neighbor. We miss the gospel when we only live a 'thou shall not' life" (p. 24). Do you agree or disagree? Why?
- Rawle makes a distinction between conviction and conversion. He explains how for Valjean, he was first convicted by the grace of M. Bienvenu, and the conversion followed. Valjean's assumptions about the world were challenged by this encounter. Rawle asks, "Can you put your finger on a time when your assumptions about the world changed?" (p. 26). Recall a time God challenged how you thought about yourself, other people, or even your faith. What happened? How did you change?
- After Valjean becomes a changed man, he has experiences where he finds it difficult to do what is right, or even to know what is right. Rawle cites several examples. Rawle writes, "First, there's the difficulty in understanding what the good is—remain hidden for the sake of others, or confess for the sake of his own soul? Second, following through with doing good is easier said than done. Although he had a powerful convicting experience, discerning and executing the good is a daily struggle. It's a daily struggle for us as well" (p. 31). Think of an instance where it was difficult to discern God's

will. How did you seek God's will? What was the result? What did you learn through that experience?

- Rawle writes, "Lenten disciplines often are framed as commitments to obedience. We fast, pray, deny, and fulfill through a joyful obedience as a child of God. Obedience may seem to be the goal, but this isn't the gospel. The goal of spiritual disciplines during Lent isn't to craft a keen sense of obedience, even though obedience is important. The point is transformation" (p. 33). How do the Christian spiritual disciplines create space in our lives for an encounter with God? How do they open us up to God's grace and the possibility of transformation?

## The Scripture

**In advance:** Use a commentary or Bible dictionary to help you prepare to discuss the Scripture. Become familiar with the text. Add questions for discussion that emerge from your study in addition to those below.

**Read aloud:** Ephesians 2:8-10

**Choose from the questions below for your discussion:**

- Ephesians 2:8-10 begins "By grace you have been saved." What is grace? How has God saved us by grace? What is the Christian story of salvation, and how is it "by grace"?
- Paul's first assertion is that we have been saved by grace. He then adds, "by faith." Faith is our response to God's action. What is faith? How do you define it? What does it mean to respond to grace with faith?
- Verse 9 says our salvation is "not the result of works, so that no one may boast." What does this mean? How do we try to take credit for our salvation? Why is it important to remember that God's action in our lives is a gift?

- What does verse 10 say concerning what God has saved us *for*? How does this animate our life in Christ? How does this claim spur us on to do good?

Conclude by reading Ephesians 2:8-10 one more time. Explain that our life with God is a gift, a result of God's gracious action toward us in Jesus. We are saved *from* sin *for* a life of good works. God has a purpose for us.

## Life Application

**Say:**

Grace is a key concept for every follower of Jesus Christ. Just as Monseigneur Myriel was gracious to Jean Valjean, so, too, has God been gracious to us in and through Jesus Christ. We have been redeemed—and at a price far exceeding the worth of silver. We have been claimed through the life, death, and resurrection of Jesus Christ.

Ask the group to reflect on how they learned about grace through their life experience. Did that experience involve a person? an event? a sermon or a book? Maybe this experience was an overwhelming gift they knew they didn't deserve. Ask the group how the lesson they learned about grace compares with what we have learned together thus far. Does the learner's experience reflect something of the grace of God? Or does the example of grace in the story of Jean Valjean and in our Scripture passage challenge the learner to rethink her or his understanding of grace? How so?

Rawle challenges us to live in light of the grace we have received. He acknowledges that this is not always easy. It is not always easy to know and do what is right. Invite each person to identify *one way* she or he can demonstrate grace to others in the week to come. Invite them to share their ideas aloud. You may want to ask group members to record their ideas on a piece of paper or a note card, and to begin the next session by asking group members to review their personal applications and see how they did.

# GO: EQUIPPED TO SERVE THE WORLD (10 MINUTES)

## A Final Thought

**Say:**

God is gracious, offering us love and mercy freely and abundantly. We see God's grace on display in Jesus, who demonstrated the meaning of grace in word and deed. We are called to follow God. Like Jean Valjean, we have had an encounter with grace. For some of us, this may be the first time we have realized how gracious God has been to us. Together, let's help one another to become a people of grace. Let's encourage one another to speak words of love and kindness, even when they aren't earned or deserved. Let's inspire one another to do good as friends of Jesus. Let's offer guidance to one another in discerning what is right. Let's be people who have received grace well, and, as a result, are forever changed.

## Closing Prayer

*Lord Jesus, we find grace in you. Teach us to walk according to your way. Send the Holy Spirit. Fill us, empower us, and embolden us, leading us to do the will of God, receiving your grace and always choosing that which is pleasing in your sight. Amen.*

## Session 2

# WHEN GRACE AND JUSTICE COLLIDE: THE STORY OF JAVERT

## SESSION OVERVIEW

### Introduction

In *Les Misérables*, Jean Valjean is a person we can identify with. He has done wrong and faced hardship, but he seeks to change and become a person who does what is right. We gravitate toward his story and want him to change. But Valjean is opposed by a policeman named Javert who believes people cannot change. Javert pursues Valjean throughout the story, utterly convinced that justice demands that Valjean be returned to prison.

Javert does everything he can to keep and maintain order, but in his stringent commitment to enforcing the law he fails to leave room for grace. We can be guilty of the same thing. How do we strike the balance? Or could it be that justice and grace are one and the same?

## Lesson Aim

*To examine the tension we encounter between the letter
and spirit of God's commands and to learn ways
of navigating those tensions in a way that honors Christ*

## Session Themes

- To explore the complexity of ethical decision making;
- To consider contemporary instances of "improvisation" where we honor the law by pursuing the spirit rather than *only* the letter of a command;
- To contemplate biblical and theological understandings of justice;
- To engage with contemporary biblical examples that push us beyond simplistic rule-keeping and into a life of holiness that grapples with complexities while relying on the Holy Spirit;
- To consider how our relationships, with God and with others, rather than strict interpretations of the law, should govern how we live.

## Chapter Focus: Javert

In each chapter, Matt Rawle explores characters, settings, and themes from *Les Misérables* to illustrate important biblical and theological truths. In this session, focus your group on the example of Javert, whose life is defined by his own understanding of right and wrong.

Javert is the primary antagonist in *Les Misérables*. He is a career law enforcement professional, serving first as a prison guard and later as a police inspector. He is very good at his job. Javert is not evil, or even a villain. Instead, he is a tragic figure. Javert is consumed by his desire to punish Jean Valjean for his crimes and becomes obsessive in his pursuit of him, even to the point of destruction. He is legalistic, maintaining a strict view of the law, seeing its enforcement as the only way of ensuring order.

## Key Scripture

*Continue in what you have learned and firmly believed, knowing from whom you learned it, and how from childhood you have known the sacred writings that are able to instruct you for salvation through faith in Christ Jesus. All scripture is inspired by God and is useful for teaching, for reproof, for correction, and for training in righteousness, so that everyone who belongs to God may be proficient, equipped for every good work.*

*(2 Timothy 3:14-17)*

## Theological Focus

Jesus was well aware of the Law. Saying "You have heard that it was said, . . . but I say to you" is not a means of throwing away the Law or treating it as unimportant. In a way, Jesus is recalibrating us to God's will by setting the Law on the scales of his own divine authority and setting the counter to God's intention as a zero point.

*(Rawle, p. 49)*

# GATHER (10 MINUTES)

Welcome the group. Ask group members if they had an opportunity to demonstrate grace to others since your last meeting. Encourage those who kept their commitments to share their experiences and to reflect theologically on how these actions honored Jesus.

Transition the group to a time of prayer.

## Opening Prayer

*Gracious God, you are a God of order and justice. You have given us your commands, and they are intended for our good. But there are times that keeping your Law becomes difficult, and we struggle*

19

*in discerning how best to honor the spirit of your commands, and not only the letter. Help us to learn how to do so. Keep us far from the sin of legalism, and instead teach us the ways of your grace; in Jesus' name. Amen.*

## Conversation Starter

**Say:**

> The second chapter in our book explores the theme of justice through an examination of the character of Javert. Most of us understand the concepts of right and wrong, or law-keeping and law-breaking. We want to acknowledge that keeping the commandments is not always simple. Sometimes we are faced with complex ethical situations, and we need God's help in doing what is right. God's commands involve both "spirit" and "letter"; there is the intention of the commandments and then the application of those commands according to how they are written. Today we will explore how to best discern and keep the spirit of the Law while respecting the letter of the Law by looking to Jesus, who models for us the way of grace.

**Ask and discuss:**

- Matt Rawle mentions that Javert is like a computer, rigidly running a program of justice and ignoring the particularities of people and circumstances in his attempts to enforce the law. Do you identify with Javert? Why or why not?
- How do you define justice? Why?
- How does your faith shape your understanding of mercy and punishment? Have you experienced ethical and moral complexities that have led you to think more carefully or deeply about how your faith informs your understanding of justice? What happened?

# GROW IN GRACE: VIDEO, BOOK, AND SCRIPTURE (40 MINUTES)

*This section allows approximately thirty minutes for discussion of the book and Scripture after the video portion concludes. You will not have time to address every discussion question. Select questions in advance you believe will be most helpful for your group and address those questions first. It may help to put a checkmark by the questions you want to cover. If time allows, incorporate additional questions.*

## Watching the Video

**Say:**

> We will continue our time together with a video featuring Matt Rawle. Matt will talk about the primary theme of our session today: justice and Javert. Notice how he explains this theme. Make connections to what we have read together in his book. Then, we will discuss both the video and our book together.

**Play the video:** Session II on Javert (approximately 10 minutes)

**Say:**

> Let's keep what Matt has said in mind as we take a look at the book and examine these themes in light of our calling to live as disciples of Jesus.

## The Book

Chapter 2 explores the theme of justice as seen in the life of Javert. Is "law and order," as a concept, good and helpful? How? When does mercy prevail over strict law-keeping? How are such judgments made, and why? Rawle invites us to reflect on God's commands and how we keep to the spirit of the commandments while honoring the letter, pointing us to Jesus Christ as our example and guide.

### Choose from the questions below for your discussion:

- How do we learn to discern right from wrong? How does Christian teaching shape our vision of justice? How does the Law provide order, and where does mercy factor in our efforts to honor and keep the Law?
- What is a wise way of approaching complex ethical dilemmas? How does the Wesleyan quadrilateral help us understand our doctrine with the help of Scripture, reason, tradition, and experience?
- Matt Rawle writes, "It's too simple to see Javert as the villain and Valjean as the hero. *Les Misérables* is much too complex to be boiled down to such a simple polarity. Javert is a beautiful foil to Valjean's seemingly murky morality. Javert is an antagonist for sure, but hardly a villain" (p. 43). Do you agree or disagree? Why?
- Rawle states, "Order is helpful, and chaos can make life more difficult, but both in their extremes make the gospel difficult to live out and share. On the one hand, having too much order makes it extremely difficult to incorporate improvisation when met with the unexpected. Likewise, having not enough order makes even the simplest of tasks exhausting" (p. 44). How can enforcing the letter of law be helpful? How can it be unhelpful? Cite examples.
- Rawle claims that the Pharisees have a lot in common with Javert. What do you know about the Pharisees? What do they have in common with Javert?
- Rawle asks, "Have you had experience with the tension between following the letter of the law versus the spirit of the law?" (p. 46). When? What happened? How did you resolve the tension?
- Rawle states, "Our assumptions about the world make things

simple. At best our assumptions help us quickly navigate the complex. . . . Assumptions can be very helpful in navigating things, but assumptions are not always helpful when working with people" (p. 48). How does the grand story of Scripture help provide a "big picture" for us in navigating our daily lives? How do particular circumstances, at times, create occasions where we must rethink our assumptions?

- Rawle observes that Javert resorts to deception in order to ensnare Jean Valjean, while Jean Valjean shifts his identity in order to do what he believes is right and good. Rawle writes, "Javert disguising himself as a beggar in order to bring Valjean to justice is like King Saul taking off his kingly garments and hiding himself in order to find solace on the eve of battle. Have you ever 'disguised' yourself? Have you ever hidden something about yourself in order to reach a desired conclusion?" (p. 52). Like these characters, we find ourselves tempted to do the "wrong thing" while saying it is for "the right reason." We are acting under the assumption that the end justifies the means. Is this way of pursuing justice moral and ethical? Why or why not?

- The climactic encounter between Jean Valjean and Javert is incredibly powerful and proves deeply unsettling for Javert. Rawle writes, "Has your worldview ever radically changed? Have you been living your life under one set of rules to discover later that you weren't as enlightened as you thought?" (p. 58). What happened? How did this experience recast your faith in God?

## The Scripture

**In advance:** Use a commentary or Bible dictionary to help you prepare to discuss the Scripture. Become familiar with the text. Add questions for discussion that emerge from your study in addition to those below.

**Read aloud:** 2 Timothy 3:14-17

**Choose from the questions below for your discussion:**

- What are your general observations about this passage?
- Paul tells Timothy that the Scriptures have been inspired "for training in righteousness" (verse 16). What is the meaning of the term *righteousness*? When is keeping God's commands and encouraging others to do the same a "righteous" endeavor? Can an effort to encourage "righteousness" in others ever result in harm? Why or why not?
- In the New Revised Standard Version, verse 15 tells us that the Scriptures "instruct" us for salvation. Compare: in the Common English Bible, verse 15 states that the Scriptures "help" us "be wise in a way that leads to salvation through faith that is in Christ Jesus." How do the Scriptures offer instruction and wisdom for us not only regarding our salvation, but also "for teaching, for reproof, for correction, and for training in righteousness"? How is training in Scripture helpful for daily living as a Christian?
- How does the example of Jesus and the guidance of the Holy Spirit help us apply the Scriptures?

Conclude by reflecting on the relationship between God's commandments given in Scripture and how they instruct us in our pursuit of justice. How do we maintain the spirit of the law while not ignoring the letter? How do we maintain justice while acting with mercy? What is the role of the Spirit in helping us? How does Jesus' example guide us?

## Life Application

**Say:**

As Christians we are called to the way of wisdom in discerning right from wrong, but we must always be loving in our pursuit of justice. Matt Rawle writes, "Our love of God informs our love of neighbor, and our love of neighbor offers a holy context to our love of God. This love is who Jesus was—fully human and fully divine—God with a face" (p. 59). Javert was cold and calculating, but as Rawle notes, "names carry nuance" (p. 43). The application of justice involves particular people with particular circumstances and should be lovingly carried out in light of the gospel.

This week, invite group members to keep their eyes open for stories that illustrate the meaning of justice. They may find a story on the news, in a magazine, on the radio, or as part of the plot of a movie or television show. In considering their example, invite group members to ask: Was justice done? Was the letter of the law strictly applied? Did the outcome also honor the "spirit" or intent of the law? Was there room for mercy? Lastly, would you rule differently in light of your faith? Why or why not?

# GO: EQUIPPED TO SERVE THE WORLD (10 MINUTES)

## A Final Thought

**Say:**

Christians should have firm convictions about justice, just like Javert. But our pursuit of justice differs because of Jesus. Justice is one of the great themes of the Bible, and the commandments were given so the people of God would live "set apart," or holy before God. Holiness is far more than keeping and enforcing rules. "Righteousness" involves living in a way that honors God in all of our circumstances, even in complex situations where it is difficult to decide what is right. The Scriptures, prayer, the guidance of the Holy Spirit, and the example of Jesus help us discern the way forward. Our pursuit of justice is recast by a collision with grace.

## Closing Prayer

*God, you are just and you know what is right. Make us into people who keep your commands, but do so in a way that always honors you. Help us always reflect your grace, your mercy, your understanding. May we never shy away from the truth or refrain from doing what is right. May we be bold, courageous, and strong, but also meek, merciful, and kind. Amen.*

# Session 3

# THE POOR ARE ALWAYS WITH YOU: THE STORY OF FANTINE

## SESSION OVERVIEW

### Introduction

A major theme of *Les Misérables* is poverty and the injustices that lead to it. As Christians, we have a calling to serve the poor, seek the lost, bind up wounds, release captives, offer healing, announce forgiveness, visit the prisoner, feed the hungry, and provide drink for the thirsty, proclaiming and demonstrating "the kingdom" Jesus preached and inaugurated.

Through the story of Fantine, Victor Hugo sheds a bright spotlight on the sufferings of the poor. Fantine's story raises questions about what is right and wrong, the importance of a strong social fabric, and the pain of injustice. Stories like Fantine's are unfolding in our world today. Do we see the poor? Do we care? They are with us. Are we with them? Do we observe Jesus' teaching, or not?

## Lesson Aim

*To awaken to the realities of poverty and injustice
surrounding us and to seek to serve others
in the name of Jesus*

## Session Themes

- To reflect on poverty and related issues through the stories of Fantine, the Thénardiers, and Gavroche;
- To accept and observe Jesus' command to love and serve "the least of these";
- To name diverse factors that contribute to poverty, including greed, selfishness, and injustice;
- To see and serve Christ through encounters with those who are poor.

## Chapter Focus: Fantine

In each chapter, Matt Rawle explores characters, settings, and themes from *Les Misérables* to illustrate important biblical and theological truths. In this session, focus your group on the example of Fantine, whose life was crushed by injustice and poverty.

Fantine enters *Les Misérables* as a beautiful young woman whose life is full of promise. But that does not last long. Fantine becomes pregnant after a relationship with a young aristocrat, who then abandons her. She is stigmatized as a single mother after the birth of her daughter, Cosette. Fantine is extorted by the family she hires to care for her daughter and later ostracized and shamed when her status as an unwed mother becomes known. She becomes impoverished and eventually resorts to prostitution to survive. She suffers greatly, and her story raises many questions about the causes of poverty and the failings of a society.

## Key Scripture

*"Then they also will answer, 'Lord, when was it that we saw you hungry or thirsty or a stranger or naked or sick or in prison, and did not take care of you?' Then he will answer them, 'Truly I tell you, just as you did not do it to one of the least of these, you did not do it to me.'"*

*(Matthew 25:44-45)*

## Theological Focus

Some say that God doesn't give you more than you can handle, but this is a lie. First, this terrible saying suggests that it is God doling out the difficulty. . . . Second, thinking that God doesn't give us more than we can handle doesn't lead us into asking the difficult questions as to why a single mother would have to lie about having a child in order to find a suitable job, why she has to offer everything she has to fulfill false debts, and why the city as a whole doesn't seem to care. For the citizens of Montreuil (and many who live in our own neighborhoods), poverty is punishment for poor choices, and the depravity is deserved. This is not the gospel.

*(Rawle, p. 65)*

# GATHER (10 MINUTES)

Welcome the group. Ask group members if they encountered a story in the past week that illustrated the concept of justice. What happened? Was justice done? Was there mercy? The story could be from the news or from daily life. Encourage group members to share their experiences and to reflect theologically on whether they believe the outcome in their example reflects God's justice. Why or why not?

Transition the group to a time of prayer.

## Opening Prayer

*Lord Jesus, you left behind the riches of heaven and became poor, born to an unwed mother. You entered the world, not in a palace, but in a stable. As we consider your teachings and the story of Les Misérables, we pray that we would grow in our love for those who are poor, suffering, or oppressed. We pray that you would equip us to serve. We pray that you would strengthen us in standing for justice. We pray you would give us a spirit of boldness in speaking the truth. We pray that we would encounter you by ministering to "the least of these." We ask these things in your name. Amen.*

## Conversation Starter

**Say:**

> The third chapter in our book focuses on the plight of the impoverished. Many of us have learned that Christianity should lead us to have concern for the poor. But knowing how to be in ministry with the poor with grace can be challenging. We want to meet the real, material needs of people and ask the difficult questions addressing the causes that lead to poverty in the first place.

**Ask and discuss:**

- As you consider the subject of poverty, what stories come to mind that illustrate the calling Christians have to care for those who are in need? You might think of a Bible story or a verse, but you might also recall a person who helped the poor or a member of your church who has demonstrated a faithful response. Share your example.
- What feelings do you have toward poverty and toward the poor? Be honest. Are you compassionate or cold? Are you concerned or indifferent? Are you afraid or driven to help? Why?

# GROW IN GRACE: VIDEO, BOOK, AND SCRIPTURE (40 MINUTES)

*This section allows approximately thirty minutes for discussion of the book and Scripture after the video portion concludes. You will not have time to address every discussion question. Select questions in advance you believe will be most helpful for your group and address those questions first. It may help to put a checkmark by the questions you want to cover. If time allows, incorporate additional questions.*

## Watching the Video

**Say:**

> We will continue our time together with a video featuring Matt Rawle. Matt will talk about the primary themes of our session today: the poor and faithful Christian witness. Notice how he explains these themes using examples from *Les Misérables*. Make connections to what we have read together in his book. Then, we will discuss both the video and our book together.

**Play the video:** Session III on Fantine (approximately 10 minutes)

**Say:**

> Let's keep what Matt has said in mind as we take a look at the book and examine these themes in light of our calling to live as disciples of Jesus.

## The Book

Chapter 3 explores an unnamed yet present character in *Les Misérables*: poverty. Victor Hugo tells the stories of Fantine, Cosette, the Thénardiers, and Gavroche so that we *look* at the poor and *enter* life with them. These stories raise many questions about the causes leading to poverty, the structure of society, and the nature of justice. They raise questions not only in the world of the story, but in our lives. Jesus did the same. He entered human history by putting on flesh and becoming poor. He identified with "the least of these." He also ministered to the poor, demonstrating for his followers the nature of God's reign. In both example and teaching, Jesus calls us to care for the poor.

**Choose from the questions below for your discussion:**

- What causes poverty? What stories are told in society and culture that explain the realities of the poor? Are these stories accurate? Or do they require further nuance? What is your explanation for poverty?
- Matt Rawle writes, "One of the main characters that affects everything in the story doesn't have a name. This character ties all of the other characters together. To some this character is avoided at all costs, for others it is the catalyst for revolution. This character is poverty itself" (p. 61). Is there a single character or example in *Les Mis* that you think best illustrates the effects of poverty? Which one? Why?
- How does your church community serve the needs of the poor? Rawle notes his congregation's service with the Louisiana Methodist Children's Home. Does your church have an ongoing ministry to the poor, widows, orphans, or others in distress?
- Rawle states, "Some say that God doesn't give you more than you can handle, but this is a lie" (p. 65). Do you agree or disagree? Why?
- Rawle discusses the Thénardiers and the deceit and darkness that emanate from them. Hugo's story causes us to long for justice. We want the Thénardiers to be found out and exposed. Rawle asks, "Do we get what we deserve? Have you ever been jealous of those who have made poor decisions,

and yet everything seems to work out? Have you felt that no good deed goes unpunished?" (p. 71). What does our longing for justice reveal to us about human nature? What does it reveal to us about God? Is there a connection between our understanding of God and our longing for justice? Explain.

- Rawle describes the Thénardiers as "hungry ghosts" (p. 72). What is a faithful Christian response to those who only know how to take? Is it possible to lovingly tell a person no? What is a Christian approach to setting healthy boundaries?
- Can helping another person ever result in harm? Does charity ever enable another person to continue in poor choices? What is a wise Christian approach to discernment in such cases? How does one learn to help others in healthy, life-giving ways?
- Rawle asks, "Have you ever been told that there's nothing you can offer? Do you think your past negates any future good that you can offer?" (p. 76). How does God's grace renew us and offer us a chance to leave our past behind and enter a new future with new possibilities?

## The Scripture

**In advance:** Use a commentary or Bible dictionary to help you prepare to discuss the Scripture. Become familiar with the text. Add questions for discussion that emerge from your study in addition to those below.

**Read aloud:** Matthew 25:31-46

**Choose from the questions below for your discussion:**

- What are your general observations about this passage?
- Jesus tells this parable to illustrate the importance of caring for "the least of these" (verses 40, 45). What kinds of people does Jesus call us to serve?

- How do we meet Christ in "the least of these"? What does this look like in practice?
- Matt Rawle observes, "According to this parable, the consequences are great in turning a blind eye to the poor" (p. 66). How is care and concern for the poor a sign of an authentic faith in Jesus? How do our deeds demonstrate that we recognize and honor Jesus as Lord?
- What does this passage reveal to us about God? How does God feel about "the least of these"? What does this mean for our discipleship to Jesus?

Conclude by reflecting on poverty and your response. How do you act differently because of Jesus' instruction to care for the poor? How does your church respond?

Consider and ask if your church fellowship is connecting with, serving, and living life alongside the poor. Where do you see this taking place? Where does your church do this well? What *could* you do to better meet the needs of those who are suffering in your town or city? Prayerfully consider ways God may be calling you, individually and collectively, to respond to the needs of your neighbors.

## Life Application

Say:

> One of the signs that we have understood the grace of God given to us in Jesus is by caring for the poor. In 2 Corinthians 8:9, Paul writes, "You know the generous act of our Lord Jesus Christ, that though he was rich, yet for your sakes he became poor, so that by his poverty you might become rich."
>
> We have a vast inheritance in Christ. Thus, even if we have little in terms of material possessions, we still have much to offer through presence, witness, service, and love. The gospel reminds us to lay down our lives in service to our neighbors. But in order to serve our neighbors and show

them the love of God, we must know them. We are called to be good neighbors to those who are poor. How do we do it?

Invite your group to seek an opportunity this week to be in ministry with the poor. This can take several forms. A group member could donate food to the food pantry or pass on gently used clothing items to those who have need. They could take someone to lunch and pick up the bill for a person they know is financially struggling. They could visit a shelter or a nursing home and simply be present with people as a listening ear and a friend. Encourage creativity. Sometimes it's as simple as listening to someone else's story. Tell group members that they will have the opportunity to share their experiences the next time you gather.

## GO: EQUIPPED TO SERVE THE WORLD (10 MINUTES)

### A Final Thought

**Say:**

Proverbs 22:9 says, "Those who are generous are blessed, / for they share their bread with the poor."

Seek an opportunity this week to share what you have with those who are poor. Be a blessing. See Christ in the other. Demonstrate love.

### Closing Prayer

*Holy Spirit, make us bold. Give us wisdom and help us grow in grace, and as we do so, show us where we can meet the needs of others. You have blessed us abundantly in your Son. May we be grateful for the gifts of eternal and abundant life that we have through him and demonstrate our gratitude through charity and love. Amen.*

## Session 4

# THE GIFT OF LOVE: THE STORY OF MARIUS AND COSETTE

## SESSION OVERVIEW

### Introduction

Love is a primary theme that runs through the heart of many of our greatest stories. *Les Misérables* is no exception, and because of this, there are many connections to the Christian faith. Matt Rawle writes, "Love is the beginning and the ending of God's story, from Creation to Resurrection to re-creation" (p. 100). Therefore, wherever love is found, there will be a thread that can be traced to the story of God. In this session we will explore the relationship between Marius and Cosette and see how their story points us to truths about the character and actions of God.

## Lesson Aim

*To discover the ways love plays an important role
in the story of Marius and Cosette and to find places
where their story illumines or connects with a robust
understanding of the love of God*

## Session Themes

- To examine love as presented in *Les Misérables* and in the Christian story;
- To explore our own understandings of love, including what it is, how it is given, and how it is received;
- To consider biblical definitions of love and integrate those definitions into our understanding of love;
- To identify practical ways of showing and sharing Christian love with others.

## Chapter Focus: Marius and Cosette

In each chapter, Matt Rawle explores characters, settings, and themes from *Les Misérables* to illustrate important biblical and theological truths. In this session, focus your group on the example of Marius and Cosette and their experiences of love.

Cosette is the daughter of Fantine. Her story is one of longing and hope; and the reader, knowing her family background, desires to see Cosette find love and happiness. Marius is a French Romantic who leaves behind the privilege of the aristocratic class to make his own way in the world. Marius falls in love with Cosette and eventually wins her heart. Cosette and Marius introduce a romantic element into the story of *Les Misérables*, raising questions about the meaning of love.

## Key Scripture

*Now faith, hope, and love abide, these three; and the greatest of these is love.*

(*1 Corinthians 13:13*)

## Theological Focus

Love is the one thing we can experience that defies time or circumstance. Love is the beginning and the ending of God's story, from Creation to Resurrection to re-creation. Too often we like to start God's story with Genesis 3 (God's punishment for eating the fruit of the tree of the knowledge of good and evil) and end it with Revelation 20 (death and judgment), but if you extend the story on either side you will see that our story is one of love.

(*Rawle, p. 100*)

# GATHER (10 MINUTES)

Welcome the group. Ask group members if they had an opportunity to forgive another person in the past week. Ask also if they found reconciliation. Lastly, ask if they found a space to work for justice in the world and thought about how to respond in a manner that accords with the "revolution" of Jesus. Did they follow through? Encourage group members to share their experiences and reflect theologically on how God teaches us to see the world differently through participation in God's kingdom.

Transition the group to a time of prayer.

## Opening Prayer

*Dear God, we often hear that you are a God of love. Some in our midst can testify that they have experienced your love or have come to understand your love through faith in Jesus. Help us grow in our understanding of love, for we know that if we are your people, the*

*world should look upon us and say, "See how they love one another."*
*Teach us and give us grace, so that we may love as you love. Amen.*

## Conversation Starter

**Say:**

> The fourth chapter in our book explores the idea of love.
> The story of Marius and Cosette raises many questions
> about what love is, how it is experienced, and how it is
> expressed. What is love? The Bible examines the very same
> question, and one of the central claims of the Christian
> tradition concerns the love of God. First John 4:16 says,
> "God is love, and those who abide in love abide in God, and
> God abides in them." John 3:16, a verse familiar to so many,
> says, "God so loved the world that he gave his only Son, so
> that everyone who believes in him may not perish but may
> have eternal life."

**Ask and discuss:**

- What is love? How did you form your definition? Are there
  other stories told today about the nature and character of
  love? What are they?
- Christians say, "God is love." What does this mean? How is
  God "love"?

# GROW IN GRACE: VIDEO, BOOK, AND SCRIPTURE (40 MINUTES)

*This section allows approximately thirty minutes for discussion
of the book and Scripture after the video portion concludes. You will
not have time to address every discussion question. Select questions in
advance you believe will be most helpful for your group and address
those questions first. It may help to put a checkmark by the questions
you want to cover. If time allows, incorporate additional questions.*

## Watching the Video

**Say:**

> We will continue our time together with a video featuring Matt Rawle. Matt will talk about the primary theme of our session today: love. Notice how he explains this idea using *Les Misérables*. Make connections to what we have read together in his book. Then, we will discuss both the video and our book together.

**Play the video:** Session IV on Marius and Cosette (approximately 10 minutes)

**Say:**

> Let's keep what Matt has said in mind as we take a look at the book and examine these themes in light of our calling to live as disciples of Jesus.

## The Book

One of the great longings of the human heart is to know and experience true love. Stories of romantic love are prominent in music, literature, and film, but there are other forms of love. There is friendship love and familial love, as well as *agape* love, or the self-giving love often associated with God. In the fourth chapter, Matt Rawle examines the love that exists between Marius and Cosette. We learn of how they encounter one another, how they fall in love, and how their love grows. We also learn of the complications present in their relationship and the obstacles they overcome that offer us the hope that we, too, might find love.

Christians also have a particular understanding of love. First John 4:10 says, "In this is love, not that we loved God but that he loved us and sent his Son to be the atoning sacrifice for our sins," and 1 John 4:19 adds simply, "We love because he first loved us."

God's love is received through Jesus and then shared. We love others because we have been first transformed by the love of God.

**Choose from the questions below for your discussion:**

- Our session began with questions about our definition of love. After hearing from Matt Rawle, is there anything you would add, amend, or change regarding your understanding of love?
- How does God reveal love to us? Where do we see God's love active and at work in our world?
- How does the love of God change and transform us? How does receiving love from God lead us to give our love back to God? How does receiving love from God lead us to love our neighbors differently than we would otherwise?
- What are hallmarks of Christian love? What characteristics demonstrate love in a way that is reflective of Jesus Christ?
- Rawle asks, "What fills your prayers? What miracles are you expecting from a God that relentlessly seeks for us?" (p. 86). How do our hopes reveal to us the presence of God's love? How does God's love for us lead us to become people of hope?
- Rawle states, "Forgetting our wounds does little to erase them. What truly defines who we are as Christians is how our wounds are healed" (p. 90). Does God use our wounds to help us become better witnesses to God's love? How does God do so?
- Rawle tells us of how itineracy as a United Methodist minister has taught him to identify more closely with Abraham and has helped him deepen his understanding of faith. How does God's faithfulness *show* us God's love? How does God's love toward us *increase* our faith?
- In John 15:13, Jesus says, "No one has greater love than this, to lay down one's life for one's friends." How does sacrificial action demonstrate love? How has God shown us love through sacrificial action? How do we show love through sacrificial action?

## The Scripture

**In advance:** Use a commentary or Bible dictionary to help you prepare to discuss the Scripture. Become familiar with the text. Add questions for discussion that emerge from your study in addition to those below.

**Read aloud:** 1 Corinthians 13:1-13

**Choose from the questions below for your discussion:**

- What are your general observations about this passage?
- Is there anything in Paul's description of love that you find surprising? challenging? difficult? Why?
- Paul presents love as an "acid test" of a vibrant relationship with God. He writes, "If I speak in the tongues of mortals and of angels, but do not have love, I am a noisy gong or a clanging cymbal" (verse 1). Paul is addressing a controversy among the church at Corinth. Some thought they were special, or superior, because of their spiritual gifts. Paul says it is love, not speaking in tongues, that truly matters. How is love a sign that God is present, active, and at work in particular situations?
- Mark 12:28-31 says, "One of the scribes came near and heard them disputing with one another, and seeing that he answered them well, he asked him, 'Which commandment is the first of all?' Jesus answered, 'The first is, "Hear, O Israel: the Lord our God, the Lord is one; you shall love the Lord your God with all your heart, and with all your soul, and with all your mind, and with all your strength." The second is this, "You shall love your neighbor as yourself." There is no other commandment greater than these.'" Jesus names love of God and love of neighbor as the greatest commandment, binding the two together. How do we love God? How do we love our neighbor? What is the connection between the two?

- Jesus says in John 13:35, "By this everyone will know that you are my disciples, if you have love for one another." When followers of Jesus love one another, how does that lend credibility to the good news message of Christ?

Conclude by reflecting on love. What is the meaning of love? How do we receive love, and how do we give it? How does our faith result in our becoming people who love God and love others?

## Life Application

**Say:**

> This week our group has explored our understanding of love and sought to deepen our understanding of love in light of our relationship to Jesus Christ.
>
> As a group, let's share concrete actions that demonstrate the kind of love that comes from God.
>
> What is something we can do that shows love? How is love expressed toward God? How is love expressed toward our neighbors? What do we do?

When someone generates an idea, you may want to ask, "How does that action connect to faith in Jesus?" Listening, service, generosity, hospitality, intercessory prayer, worship, studying Scripture, gathering in fellowship, visiting the sick, caring for widows and orphans, speaking against injustice, and many other actions have direct connections to Christian discipleship. Help people make those connections so that they can better understand what it means to live a life of love.

As you send group members forth, invite them to commit to one act of love that they will do in the week ahead.

# GO: EQUIPPED TO SERVE THE WORLD (10 MINUTES)

## A Final Thought

Say:

> God is a God of love. We see this foremost in Jesus Christ. God has extended love to us by redeeming us and rescuing us from the power of sin and death. As recipients of God's love, we are given the opportunity to share God's love with others. Together, let's give witness to the love of God. Through our witness, may others also "taste and see that the LORD is good" (Psalm 34:8).

## Closing Prayer

*Loving God, help us to love all people in your name. Help us to be patient, kind, long-suffering, and committed to the truth. May we leave behind childish ways and mature in your love, knowing deeply and fully that your love for us is sure and unshakable, and, standing in the confidence that we are loved, may we extend that same love to people of every tribe, tongue, and nation with humility, respect, and gentleness. We ask all this in Jesus' name. Amen.*

# Session 5

# BUILDING THE BARRICADE: THE STORY OF *LES AMIS*

## SESSION OVERVIEW

### Introduction

*Les Misérables* is a historical novel, a fact that is preserved in the various adaptations that have been made for stage and screen. In the story we encounter Valjean, Javert, Fantine, Cosette, and many others. But we also learn a great deal about the history of France: the architecture, geography, and the conflicts between the French monarchy and the everyday citizen. In *Les Misérables*, the concept of revolution becomes a major element of the plot, as several characters are caught up in a movement calling for societal change.

This theme connects to the story of Jesus. How are the people of God called to bring about change in the world? Jesus came announcing the kingdom of God, an alternative to the kingdoms of this world. What is this revolution we've been called to join? Jesus' revolution differs from the revolutions of this world. His ways are not our ways. Jesus came to bring peace, and we are called to be heralds and witnesses to that peace, won for us on the cross.

## Lesson Aim

*To heed the call to repudiate violence against fellow human beings when working for justice and to imagine alternative ways of peaceful action that are rooted in the gospel and made possible in and through Jesus Christ*

## Session Themes

- To name the struggles against oppression and injustice that exist today;
- To understand ways Jesus may have been understood as a revolutionary in the first century;
- To examine the revolutionary conflict in *Les Misérables* and see how it serves as an example of how well-intentioned movements can lead to violence and loss;
- To consider ways in which Jesus has offered us an alternative way of peace that rejects violence and works gently, humbly, and patiently for justice;
- To explore the practice of peacemaking.

## Chapter Focus: Friends of the ABC

In each chapter, Matt Rawle explores characters, settings, and themes from *Les Misérables* to illustrate important biblical and theological truths. In this session, focus your group on the example of Friends of the ABC and their experience of calling for revolution.

The Friends of the ABC challenge the French monarchy by advocating for a republican form of government. The monarchy and the aristocratic class are blamed for the problems of French society. In *Les Misérables*, the Friends of the ABC claim to be on the side of the poor and oppressed. They believe new leadership would yield a more just society. Their efforts lead to a street fight between their sympathizers and the French National Guard. The French National Guard are victorious, and the revolutionaries are crushed. Rawle parallels elements of the *Les Mis* story with the story of Jesus and challenges us to imagine ways to work for peace that reject violence.

## Key Scripture

*"You have heard that it was said, 'You shall love your neighbor and hate your enemy.' But I say to you, Love your enemies and pray for those who persecute you, so that you may be children of your Father in heaven; for he makes his sun rise on the evil and on the good, and sends rain on the righteous and on the unrighteous. For if you love those who love you, what reward do you have? Do not even the tax collectors do the same? And if you greet only your brothers and sisters, what more are you doing than others? Do not even the Gentiles do the same? Be perfect, therefore, as your heavenly Father is perfect."*

*(Matthew 5:43-48)*

## Theological Focus

Love of God and love of neighbor should always be our motivation as followers of Christ, and the way we share the core of our faith in the world is through multiplying fruitfulness. But sin is tempting because it is so close to being right.

*(Rawle, p. 114)*

# GATHER (10 MINUTES)

Welcome the group. Ask group members if they were able to serve a person in an impoverished circumstance this past week, whether directly (for example, serving a meal) or indirectly (providing for others who meet the needs of the poor). How did they bless "the least of these"? Did they encounter Christ in that experience? How? Encourage group members to share their experiences and reflect theologically on how God teaches us through interactions with others.

Transition the group to a time of prayer.

## Opening Prayer

*Gracious God, you sent your Son Jesus into the world to demon-strate for us what it means to live life fully under your care. Jesus has called us to love you and to love our neighbor, and has modeled for us a different way of life, one of love, peace, and justice. But as human beings, we are prone to sin and are guilty of violence against one another. Forgive us for causing harm, and help us to learn to forgive others as we have been forgiven. Fill us with your Spirit, so that we may find the grace we need to do your will. Amen.*

## Conversation Starter

**Say:**

The fifth chapter in our book explores the idea of revolutionary change. Jesus came to change our world. But he did so through love and self-sacrifice, humility and service. To the contrary, the revolutions of our world sadly and all too often resort to violence. Often, we believe change can only be achieved through the use of force. *Les Misérables* offers a good example. The desires of the Friends of the ABC were noble. They believed that the monarchy was creating the conditions that yielded poverty and oppression, and that a republic would result in a more just society. But in fighting for their cause, the Friends of the ABC resorted to violent resistance. We often do the same. Jesus offers us an alternative.

**Ask and discuss:**

- Matt Rawle writes, "Every revolution needs at least three ingredients—a problem, a solution, and a leader. Regardless if either problem or solution is real or perceived, a revolution is meant to overthrow, overturn, destroy, or upend the way things are" (p. 104). Where do you see a call for revolution today? What causes a revolution to turn violent? Can societal change be realized apart from violence? Why or why not?

* How does discipleship to Jesus shape the ways you work for change in our world?

# GROW IN GRACE: VIDEO, BOOK, AND SCRIPTURE (40 MINUTES)

*This section allows approximately thirty minutes for discussion of the book and Scripture after the video portion concludes. You will not have time to address every discussion question. Select questions in advance you believe will be most helpful for your group and address those questions first. It may help to put a checkmark by the questions you want to cover. If time allows, incorporate additional questions.*

## Watching the Video

**Say:**

We will continue our time together with a video featuring Matt Rawle. Matt will talk about the theme of our session for today: revolution, or how to change the world. Notice how Matt makes connections among the story of Jesus, *Les Misérables*, and our world. Following the video we will discuss what we have seen, heard, and read in our book together.

**Play the video:** Session V on *Les Amis* (approximately 10 minutes)

**Say:**

Let's keep what Matt has said in mind as we take a look at the book and examine our theme in light of our calling to live as disciples of Jesus.

## The Book

Chapter 5 explores our desire for justice, societal tensions, calls for revolution, and how individuals and groups work for change. Rawle directs our attention to the contrast between revolutionary efforts like those of the Friends of the ABC and that of Jesus Christ, who demonstrated an alternative way of peace requiring self-sacrifice, forgiveness, and an openness to the hope of reconciliation. Jesus was tempted to pursue other avenues of establishing his kingdom, but he was obedient to God, taking up his cross and laying down his life for us. As Rawle states, "Meditating on the events of Jesus' last week in Jerusalem helps us rethink conventional notions of revolution" (p. 104).

**Choose from the questions below for your discussion:**

- What societal conditions lead people to call for revolutionary change? Do you think our society creates space where the needs, wants, and desires of all people can be heard and addressed? Why or why not?
- Concerning Jesus' entry into Jerusalem, Matt Rawle writes, "The crowd is shouting, 'Hosanna,' which means 'Save us!' This triumphant entry would certainly be enough to get the attention of the Roman authority, who would hear the shouts of salvation as a political referendum defying Roman occupation. The Romans aren't wrong to be fearful of an uprising. Taking Jesus' last week as a whole, it seems that the crowd was begging for a political revolution" (pp. 104–105). Do you agree with this understanding of this event? Why?
- Why was Jesus crucified? Was Jesus rightly considered a dangerous person? How did his message challenge the ruling powers of his day? How does his message challenge the ruling powers of *our* day?
- Rawle writes, "Waiting does not come easily to me. When

inspiration hits, or someone has an idea for a new ministry or project, I am very quick to jump in and move full steam ahead" (p. 106). How can moving too quickly get us into trouble? How does the way of Jesus call us to slowness, patience, thoughtfulness, and gentleness, and why should we remember this when we seek to change our world?

- The author writes, "The crowd chose Barabbas because they did not have a holy imagination to believe that Christ could change reality itself. Do we really believe in the power of Christ to upend our assumptions about the world?" (p. 118). Jesus defied the existing categories of his day, failing to align with the Sadducees, Pharisees, Essenes, or Zealots. How does the way of Jesus continue to defy our categories? Why do we struggle to believe his way can lead to peace?

- Rawle writes, "I pray for a day that we realize that only Jesus' blood needed to be spilled. I think Jesus' first words from the cross, 'Father, forgive them; for they do not know what they are doing' (Luke 23:34), are spoken over and over again when we build barricades, choose Barabbas, or think that revolution and resurrection are one and the same. Hearing Jesus say these words causes us to turn away in embarrassment. How can such grace be offered when we time and time again turn away from the Kingdom that Jesus began?" (p. 119). Do you resonate with Rawle's longing? Do you think choosing to forgive like Jesus forgave is possible for Christians? Why or why not?

- How do we become people who can forgive those who harm us?

- What can Christians do to show others it is possible to reject violent means of societal change?

## The Scripture

**In advance:** Use a commentary or Bible dictionary to help you prepare to discuss the Scripture. Become familiar with the text. Add questions for discussion that emerge from your study in addition to those below.

**Read aloud:** Matthew 5:38-48

**Choose from the questions below for your discussion:**

- What are your general observations about this passage?
- How did Jesus love his enemies and pray for his persecutors? How has Jesus shown love for *us* in unexpected ways?
- God has shown us grace through Jesus by loving us freely. We do not earn God's love. How does this change us regarding our interactions with those who oppose us? Stated differently, how does God's grace toward us lead us to show grace to others?
- What does it mean to "be perfect," as Jesus describes? John Wesley understood Christian perfection as being "'habitually filled with the love of God and neighbor' and as 'having the mind of Christ and walking as he walked.'"* What "means of grace" help us grow in Christian maturity?
- Matthew 5:9 says, "Blessed are the peacemakers, for they will be called children of God." What does it mean to be a peacemaker? What are common, everyday examples of how disciples of Jesus "make peace"?
- How do you define forgiveness? How do you extend forgiveness? How do you ask for forgiveness?
- In Colossians 3:13 Paul writes, "Bear with one another and, if anyone has a complaint against another, forgive each other; just as the Lord has forgiven you, so you also must forgive." What does this look like in practice?
- Do you find Jesus' teaching in Matthew 5:38-48 revolutionary? How does it offer an alternative vision for working toward societal change?

---

* "What Did John Wesley Mean by 'Moving on to Perfection?,'" UMC.org, June 25, 2018, http://www.umc.org/what-we-believe/what-did-john-wesley-mean -by-moving-on-to-perfection, accessed September 21, 2019.

Conclude by reflecting on Jesus and his cross. How did Jesus change the world by going to the cross? How did he demonstrate love? During the Lenten season we routinely turn toward the cross and consider again Jesus' final week, his final words, and his final action in defeating death on the cross. How does this change our way of living in the world today? How does it instruct us in how we announce and enact the peace of God? How does the revolution of Jesus differ from every other revolutionary effort?

## Life Application

**Say:**

> God calls us to stand for justice. Sometimes that may require advocacy for revolutionary change. But how we stand for justice must be done in the spirit, wisdom, and way of Jesus. It must demonstrate love for neighbor, not only for a cause. It must be seen in displays of winsomeness, humility, and love.

Invite the group to reflect on a cause or issue they are passionate about, something they would like to see change in our world. Ask, "Does this cause connect to your Christian faith? How? What do you think God wants regarding the cause you are passionate about?" Provide a piece of paper and a writing utensil, and ask members of the group to write down their cause and the change they would like to see in the world. Then ask, "What is one way you could advocate for that change in a way that honors Christ?"

It may be as simple as prayer, or as involved as organizing an event or a campaign advocating for change. It may be in the community, in the nation, or in a much smaller unit, like the family. Invite group participants to think of how their chosen course of action reflects their faith in Jesus. Is there a need for forgiveness? reconciliation?

Create time and space for the group to share their ideas with one another. It may be that there is overlap and an opportunity for creative partnership. Lastly, take time to pray for your group participants, that God would give them wisdom as they work to bring about change in the way of Christ.

## GO: EQUIPPED TO SERVE THE WORLD (10 MINUTES)

### A Final Thought

**Say:**

> In Matthew 6:9-13, Jesus teaches us to pray, "Our Father in heaven, / hallowed be your name. / Your kingdom come. / Your will be done, / on earth as it is in heaven. / Give us this day our daily bread. / And forgive us our debts, / as we also have forgiven our debtors. / And do not bring us to the time of trial, / but rescue us from the evil one." That is a powerful prayer. We pray that God will deliver us from the temptation of violent revolution and give us the grace we need to instead participate in God's revolution of love—that God's reign would come and will be done here as in heaven.

### Closing Prayer

*Lord Jesus, thank you for showing us another way to live, demonstrating forgiveness by forgiving us, then inviting us to forgive others in your name. Thank you for opening the way of reconciliation not only between God and humankind, but between people who differ from one another. We pray that you would help us to receive your grace and to extend grace to others, even to those with whom we disagree. May we love our enemies, as Christ commands, and be made perfect in your love. Amen.*

## Session 6

# THE BLESSED GARDEN: A HOPEFUL VISION

### SESSION OVERVIEW

## Introduction

Matt Rawle writes, "Much like poverty is an unnamed character in Hugo's story that unites all of the characters together, Hugo's use of gardens reveals another story just under the surface" (p. 121). In this session, we will explore the symbolism of the garden in *Les Misérables* and in the story of Scripture. Gardens can remind us of God's beauty. They can refresh us, bringing to mind our need for rest. They can also invite us to serve as cultivators and stewards of God's work in the world. Gardens are signs of grace.

## Lesson Aim

*To explore the symbolism of the garden*
*in* Les Misérables *and in Scripture and see how they serve*
*as reminders of God's grace*

## Session Themes

- To examine Victor Hugo's use of the garden in *Les Misérables*;
- To explore various garden narratives in Scripture;
- To identify ways gardens serve as signs of God's grace;
- To understand that, in and through Jesus Christ, "new creation" has begun, which God will bring to culmination and fulfillment at the end of the age.

## Chapter Focus: The Garden

In each chapter, Matt Rawle explores characters, settings, and themes from *Les Misérables* to illustrate important biblical and theological truths. In this session, focus your group on the example of the garden as presented by Victor Hugo.

Rawle observes, "Although Hugo isn't so explicit about God's story being that of three gardens, it seems that the gardens throughout *Les Misérables* are a symbol of God's presence" (p. 126). Several important moments in Hugo's story take place in a garden. Jean Valjean, for a time, even works as a gardener.

## Key Scripture

*Then the angel showed me the river of the water of life, bright as crystal, flowing from the throne of God and of the Lamb through the middle of the street of the city. On either side of the river is the tree of life with its twelve kinds of fruit, producing its fruit each month; and the leaves of the tree are for the healing of the nations. Nothing accursed will be found there any more. But the throne of God and of the Lamb will be in it, and his servants will worship him; they will see his face, and his name will be on their foreheads. And there will be no more night; they need no light of lamp or sun, for the Lord God will be their light, and they will reign forever and ever.*

*(Revelation 22:1-5)*

## Theological Focus

It is both garden and city representing heaven and earth coming together, and in this holy place we will see the face of God. God will be the only source of light, and there we will rest in God's heart for eternity. From the garden of Eden to the garden of suffering and resurrection to the city garden where all things are one, God's story has always been about a garden and our place within it.

*(Rawle, p. 126)*

# GATHER (10 MINUTES)

Welcome the group. Ask group members if they followed through on their commitments to perform an act of love in the past week. What did they do? How did it go? Did they learn anything new about God through the experience? Did a relationship grow stronger due to a loving word or deed? Invite group members to share their experiences.

Transition the group to a time of prayer.

## Opening Prayer

*Holy Spirit, come and renew us. Open our hearts and allow us to receive your word in the way good soil is receptive to a life-bearing seed. Let the love of God take hold and become rooted in us, springing up and bringing forth the fruit of love, joy, peace, patience, goodness, faithfulness, gentleness, and self-control in our lives. In the name of Jesus we pray. Amen.*

## Conversation Starter

Say:

> The sixth and final chapter in our book explores the theme of the garden. The garden is key to the story Victor Hugo

tells in *Les Misérables*. It is also key in the story of Scripture. Gardens are a sign of grace. They show us the beauty and creativity of God. They remind us to rest. They also invite us to participate as workers and cultivators, creating space for communion with God, with creation, and with others. Not only are gardens signs, they also offer us a foretaste of the new creation that has come and is coming.

In this session, we will make connections between the gardens found in *Les Misérables* and the spiritual life. We will examine places in Scripture where a garden communicates truth about who God is and what God is doing. Finally, we will be invited to live as people of hope.

**Ask and discuss:**

- Do you have a significant life memory that involves a garden? Did a family member cultivate a garden? Perhaps you grew up in an urban area and have had very little experience with gardens. If you have a memory, share it.
- What effect do gardens have on the human spirit? What is life-giving about a garden?

## GROW IN GRACE: VIDEO, BOOK, AND SCRIPTURE (40 MINUTES)

*This section allows approximately thirty minutes for discussion of the book and Scripture after the video portion concludes. You will not have time to address every discussion question. Select questions in advance you believe will be most helpful for your group and address those questions first. It may help to put a checkmark by the questions you want to cover. If time allows, incorporate additional questions.*

## Watching the Video

**Say:**

> We will continue our time together with a video featuring Matt Rawle. Matt will talk about the primary theme of our session today: the garden. Notice how he explains this theme using examples from *Les Misérables*. Make connections to what we have read together in his book. Then, we will discuss both the video and our book together.

**Play the video:** Session VI on A Hopeful Vision (approximately 10 minutes)

**Say:**

> Let's keep what Matt has said in mind as we take a look at the book and examine our theme in light of our calling to live as disciples of Jesus.

## The Book

Chapter 6 explores the theme of the garden as it is found in Victor Hugo's *Les Misérables* and in the story of Scripture. Isaiah 51:3 offers this promise:

*For the LORD will comfort Zion;*
*    he will comfort all her waste places,*
*and will make her wilderness like Eden,*
*    her desert like the garden of the LORD;*
*joy and gladness will be found in her,*
*    thanksgiving and the voice of song.*

Where there was formerly desolation, God brings joy and gladness, gratitude and singing. Matt Rawle reminds us that gardens can represent different aspects of grace, and that grace can be "wild and unexpected."

**Choose from the questions below for your discussion:**

- The Bible contains several stories involving gardens. Matt Rawle cites examples from Scripture in his book. Which biblical example connects most deeply with you? Why?
- Rawle notes that in the first Creation account given in Genesis, God brings order from chaos. In the same way that a well-kept garden offers signs of purpose, design, and intent, and thus the mind of a gardener, the Creation offers signs that point us to a Creator. Does time in nature point you to God? How? Share examples with the group.
- Just before his arrest, mock trial, and crucifixion, Jesus prays in the garden of Gethsemane. After Jesus was crucified, he is buried in a garden tomb. Rawle observes, "On the third day, Mary comes to the tomb early in the morning to find that the stone already has been rolled away. Interestingly when she first sees the risen Lord, she mistakes him as the gardener" (p. 125). What does this interaction between Jesus and Mary reveal to us about Jesus? Is Jesus a gardener? How so?
- Rawle writes, "Daily spiritual practices help keep God's grace always before us" (p. 126). One spiritual practice is the observance of Sabbath. What are your daily spiritual practices? How do they serve to remind you of and open you to God's grace?
- The author states, "Gardens are a place for Sabbath rest, but they also take a great deal of work" (p. 130). God invites us to serve as co-laborers and friends in the work God is doing in our world. Rather than working *for* God, we work *with* God. Does this encourage you? Why?
- Rawle writes, "Hugo's gardens serve as diversely beautiful backdrops reflecting characters' grounding in their relationships or the world around them. For the priest the garden represents Sabbath. For Valjean a garden is hard work. For Cosette and Marius it is wild and passionate. What is our relationship with God's creation?" (p. 134). How do you respond?

- Rawle states, "When the new heaven and the new earth become one, when God brings God's story to a close, Christ, the Lamb of God, is there offering perpetual light on all the good work that God has done. There at the end of it all, all of God's creation will come together at the foot of the tree of life for the 'healing of the nations' (Revelation 22:2). Until then there is still work to be done." (p. 139). What is our everyday work as followers of Jesus? Where do we sow seeds? Where do we create beauty? Where do we open up space for rest? How do we cultivate and steward God's creation until the day Jesus restores all things, making the new heaven and the new earth one? Be specific. What does this look like in practice?

## The Scripture

**In advance:** Use a commentary or Bible dictionary to help you prepare to discuss the Scripture. Become familiar with the text. Add questions for discussion that emerge from your study in addition to those below.

**Read aloud:** Revelation 22:1-5

**Choose from the questions below for your discussion:**

- What are your general observations about this passage?
- How does this image from Revelation offer us a hopeful vision of God's future? Would you like to dwell in the city of God? Why? Does this inspire you to invite others to share in Christian hope?
- John the Revelator describes "the tree of life" whose leaves are "for the healing of the nations" (verse 2). When we think of healing, we often think of God restoring individuals to full health. How are nations in need of healing?
- How can the church be a "sign and foretaste" of the garden standing in the city of God, described for us in Revelation? What words and actions can the church offer that give life and light to the world?

61

- The river described by John the Revelator is said to flow "from the throne of God and of the Lamb" (verse 1). Life, flourishing, and blessings have God as their source. What does this suggest about our communion with God? If we draw near to God and allow God to exercise God's rule in our lives, what might we witness flowing forth from us?

Conclude by reflecting on the meaning of the garden. How does the garden stand as a powerful symbol of hope? What does it communicate to us about God? How does this image capture our imagination and inspire us to live as followers of Jesus today?

## Life Application

**Say:**

> Matt Rawle writes:
>
> "At the end of it all, Hugo means to show that the gardens throughout *Les Misérables* represent the different aspects of grace. Sometimes grace offers peace. Sometimes offering grace takes great work. Sometimes grace is wild and unexpected. It's beautiful to ponder for a moment that we are always surrounded by God's symphony of nature. Every time we draw a breath we should give thanks for the grace God has offered to us. God's loving presence is all around us if we have eyes to see it" (pp. 136–137).
>
> As a group, you have considered the gardens of *Les Misérables* and the gardens of the Bible. What do these gardens communicate to you about God's grace? God's presence? God's activity? Does the image of the garden offer an invitation to you as a follower of Jesus Christ? Do you find God inviting you to rest? to contemplate beauty? to worship? to work, joining God in God's activity?
>
> Who is God calling you to become? How is God inviting you to grow in faith? In what ways will you seek to bless others as a servant of Jesus?

Ask group members to share the ways they connect the theme of the garden to their spiritual life. Make connections to the life of faith. How is our life like a garden, how does God tend, prune, shape, plant, and cultivate new life in us? How, then, do others encounter God's grace through our love, service, and Christlike actions?

For your final reflection, ask the group to offer the most significant insight they had concerning the Christian life while participating in this study. As a group, give thanks to God for what has been learned. Pray, asking God to help you apply these truths and put them into practice so that all group participants might continue to grow in grace.

# GO: EQUIPPED TO SERVE THE WORLD (10 MINUTES)

## A Final Thought

**Say:**

> Gardens bring to our attention several powerful truths about God and grace. In some ways, this study has served as a kind of garden, sowing seeds and cultivating in each one of us a deeper understanding of life with God. Will we bear good fruit? Will we bless others? Will we allow God to graciously work in and through us, transforming us in heart, mind, soul, and body?
>
> *May it be so.*

## Closing Prayer

*God, you are the true master gardener. Please, help us to abide in Jesus, drawing our life from him, the true vine. In John 15:8, Jesus tells us, "My Father is glorified by this, that you bear much fruit and become my disciples." May we bring you glory in all that we do. We ask this in Jesus' name. Amen.*

# The Grace of *Les Misérables*

*The Grace of Les Misérables*
978-1-5018-8710-9
978-1-5018-8711-6  eBook

*The Grace of Les Misérables / DVD*
978-1-5018-8714-7

*The Grace of Les Misérables / Leader Guide*
978-1-5018-8712-3
978-1-5018-8713-0  eBook

*The Grace of Les Misérables / Youth Study Book*
978-1-5018-8721-5
978-1-5018-8722-2  eBook

*The Grace of Les Misérables / Worship Resources*
978-1-5018-8723-9 Flash Drive
978-1-5018-8724-6 Download

*The Grace of Les Misérables / Leader Kit*
978-1-5018-8725-3